MW01710704

ENGLISH PRACTICE AND PROGRESS

GRAMMAR ACTIVITIES
(PRE-INTERMEDIATE – INTERMEDIATE)

JANE ROLLASON

SCHOLASTIC

MARY GLASGOW MAGAZINES

Contents

Unchanging World

The verbs in these fascinating facts are mixed up. Can you sort them out?

1

A koala bear **closes** for up to 22 hours each day. ______________________

2

In the summer in the Arctic Circle, the sun never **travels**. ______________________

3

An astronaut footprint on the surface of the moon **sleeps** for millions of years.

____

4

The largest flower in the world is called a Rafflesia - it **lasts** up to 7 kilos and **loses** up to 1 metre across. ______________________

5

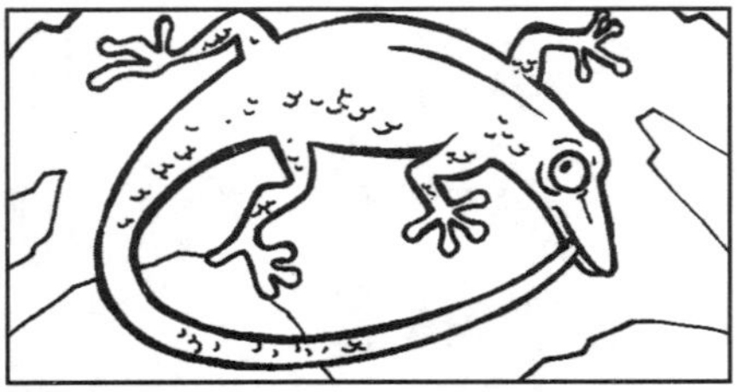

If a lizard **drinks** its tail, it grows another one. ______________________

6

In art galleries around the world, each visitor **measures** an average of three seconds in front of each painting.

____

7

In baseball, when a pitcher **beats** a good ball, it **weighs** at about 160 kilometres an hour. ______________________

8

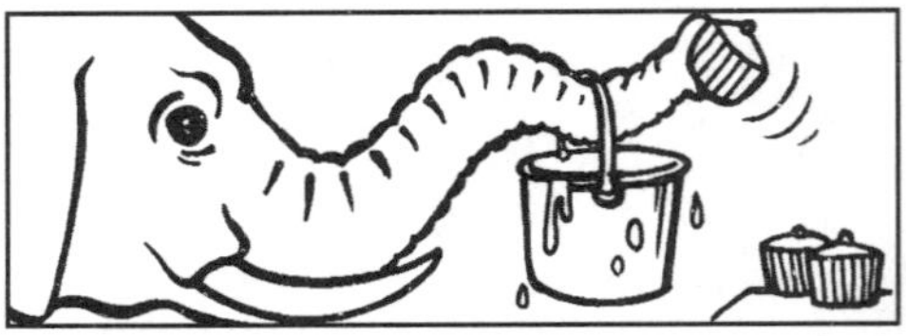

An adult elephant **spends** about 225 litres of water every day. ______________________

9

A snake never **throws** its eyes at any time. ______________________

10

A human heart **sets** about 70 times a minute. ______________________

You're Late!

It's Helen's birthday. She has invited a group of friends to go to the theatre to see a show. Her boyfriend, Rob, is late. Helen calls him on her mobile phone. Choose a verb from this box for each space in the conversation and put it in the present continuous. Use the pictures to help you.

Each time you take a verb, write the letter next to it here to find the name of the show:

___ ____ ____

fall into	n
run out of	g
push	n
leave	h
sit	e
get on	k
run	o
go into	i
drive down	i
wait	t
get out	l

Where's Your Homework?

Make sentences to go with these excuses. Use the table to help you.

My father	ate	with it.
The queen	exploded.	
An eagle	stole	and took it back to his university.
My brother	came	my school bag.
My computer	landed in our garden	with it.
Some boys	took my homework	it.
A professor	made a paper plane	to tea.
The dog	lit the fire	and took my homework back to their planet.
Aliens	thought it was brilliant	and used it to make a nest.

1 *The dog ate it.*

2 ________________

3 ________________

4 ________________

5 ________________

6 ________________

7 ________________

8 ________________

9 ________________

Michael Johnson - his feet never touch the ground

Read about Michael Johnson. Put the verbs into the past simple and fit them in the passage about him. Then, complete the grid with the verbs to find the answer to this question: What subject did Michael study at college?

say
be
realise
seem
study
break
retire
sign
win

He won 5 Olympic gold medals.

He (1) b*roke*________ 6 world records.

He ran 200 metres in 19.32 seconds and 400 metres in 43.18 seconds.

He was born in Texas and he has lived all his life there. His dad (2) w______________ a truck driver. Everybody at school was amazed by his running talent. His high school coach said that his feet never (3) s______________ to touch the ground.

He went to college and (4) s______________ for a degree. While he was at college, he (5) r______________ that he could make a career in athletics. He was world no.1 at 200m and 400m by the age of 23. At the 1996 Atlanta Olympics, Johnson was the first athlete ever to win both the 200m and the 400m finals. The 200m final was his favourite race. 'That was as close as I've ever got to the perfect race,' he (6) s______________.

He soon became one of the highest paid athletes of all time. In 1997 he (7) s______________ a 6-year deal with Nike worth $12million. He was wearing special shoes when he (8) w______________ the 400m final at the Sydney Olympics in 2000 – they had pieces of real gold sewn into them.

He (9) r______________ in 2001 at the age of 33 when he was still at the top.

3)		S			○						
2)				W	○						
9)	R				○						
1)		B	*R*	*O*	*K*	*E*					
5)				R	○						
4)				S	○						
6)			S		○						
8)			W		○						
7)			S		○						

Amazon Diary

Ben was on an expedition through the Amazon when he lost the other people in his group. Here's part of his diary. Choose the blocks of letters below and put them in the correct spaces to complete the story.

DAY 18 I HAVE LOST THE OTHERS.

DAY 20 I WAITED A

DAY. I [a] RD MANY STRANGE SOUNDS. I
HAD SO [a] CHOCOLATE AND [b] E WATER
BUT NO [a] NG ELSE. THERE [b] E ANTS
ALL OV [a] THE CHOCOLATE [b] I
BRUSHED THEM OFF. THEN T [b] RAN ALL
OVER ME, SO I [c] TO THE RIVER. I
JUM [d] INTO [c] BOAT BUT IT SANK. I
FOU [d] MYSELF [c] THE WATER.
IMM [d] ATELY I [c] S SURROUNDED BY
PIR [d] A FISH. I CLIMBED ONTO A LOG.
IT WASN'T A LOG. IT WA [e] CROCODILE.
I GRAB [f] HOLD OF A [e] NCH HANGING
OVER T [f] WATER. IT WA [e] A BRANCH.
IT WAS [f] MONKEY'S TAI [e] FELL BACK
IN THE [f] VER. I PREPARED TO DIE. BUT
THE CROCODILE ATE THE PIRAHNA FISH
AND THE MONKEY ATE THE ANTS. THEN
THE CRO [g] ILE CHASED THE MO [h] Y
AND I S [g] DOWNSTREAM AND G [h] OUT.
AND HER [g] AM, WRITING MY DI [h] I
HAVE SU [g] VED. WHAT'S THAT NO [h]
..........................AAAAAAAAAAGGGHHH!

1	2	3	4	5	6	7	8
S A	BED	PED	NKE	HEA	COD	RAN	SOM
BRA	HE	ND	OT	ME	WAM	MY	WER
SN'T	A	EDI	ARY	THI	E I	IN	BUT
L. I	RI	AHN	ISE?	ER	RVI	WA	HEY

How many different types of creature did he meet? ....

Who do you think he met at the end? ....

Pompeii

Read the text. Then, answer the questions.

Today is August 24, AD 79. We are in Pompeii, a small town in southern Italy, during the time of the Roman Empire. The town lies just below Mount Vesuvius, an ancient volcano. Farmers grow food on the slopes of the mountain.

People are busy in the town. Let's walk down the main street. First we pass a taverna. A young man is drinking a glass of wine at the bar. Next we smell fresh bread from the bakery. Two women are buying loaves and honey cakes. In the road a crowd of children are playing a game with stones. Maximus Minimus walks past – he lives behind the bakery. He invites us in. We follow him into his open air courtyard. His wife, Agrippina, is here, writing a letter. The workmen are painting pictures of the countryside on the walls. A dog is sleeping in the corner.

Suddenly there is an explosion. The sky goes dark. The ground shakes violently. There is lightning. Everybody thinks it is an earthquake, but they are wrong. It is the volcano. After 800 years, Mount Vesuvius has woken up. Fire and lava burst out of the top. Black clouds of hot ash fill the sky and the wind takes them over Pompeii. Maximus grabs Agrippina's hand and they run out of the house. The dog hides under a table. The children cry for their parents. Men, women, children and animals run through the streets. Most of them escape but two thousand die.

When it is over, the sky stays dark. Piles of ash cover everything. It looks like snow.

1. **What was the young man doing when the volcano erupted?** ________________
2. **What were the two women doing?** ________________
3. **What were the children doing?** ________________
4. **What was Agrippina doing?** ________________
5. **What were the workmen doing?** ________________
6. **What was the dog doing?** ________________
7. **What did Maximus do when the volcano erupted?** ________________
8. **What did the dog do?** ________________
9. **What did the children do?** ________________
10. **What happened to the people of Pompeii?** ________________

Memory Test

Look at this page for 1 minute.

YESTERDAY EVENING 8.30

Mark

Lulu

Julia and Marlon

THIS MORNING 11.00

THIS AFTERNOON 4.00

Now, cover this page and answer the questions on the next page.

1 What was Lulu doing at 11.00 this morning? ______________________

2 What was Mark doing at 8.30 yesterday evening? ______________________

3 What were Julia and Marlon doing at 8.30 yesterday evening? ______________________

4 When was Lulu flying a helicopter? ______________________

5 When were Julia and Marlon playing their guitars? ______________________

6 What was Lulu doing at 4.00 this afternoon? ______________________

7 What was Mark doing at 11.00 this morning? ______________________

8 When was Mark ice-skating? ______________________

9 What were Julia and Marlon doing at 11.00 this morning? ______________________

10 What was Mark doing at 4.00 this afternoon? ______________________

That's History!

Look at the timeline and answer the questions.

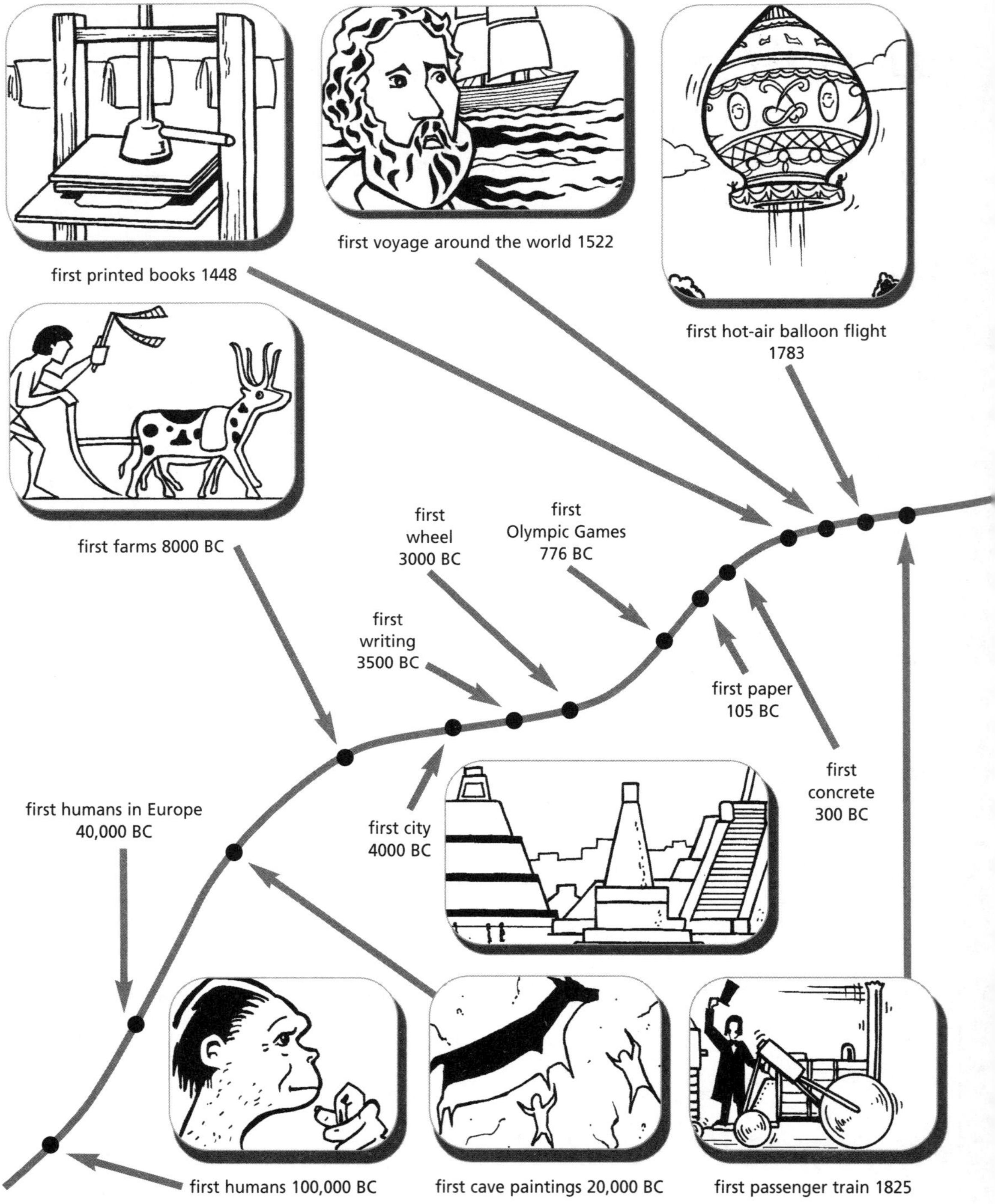

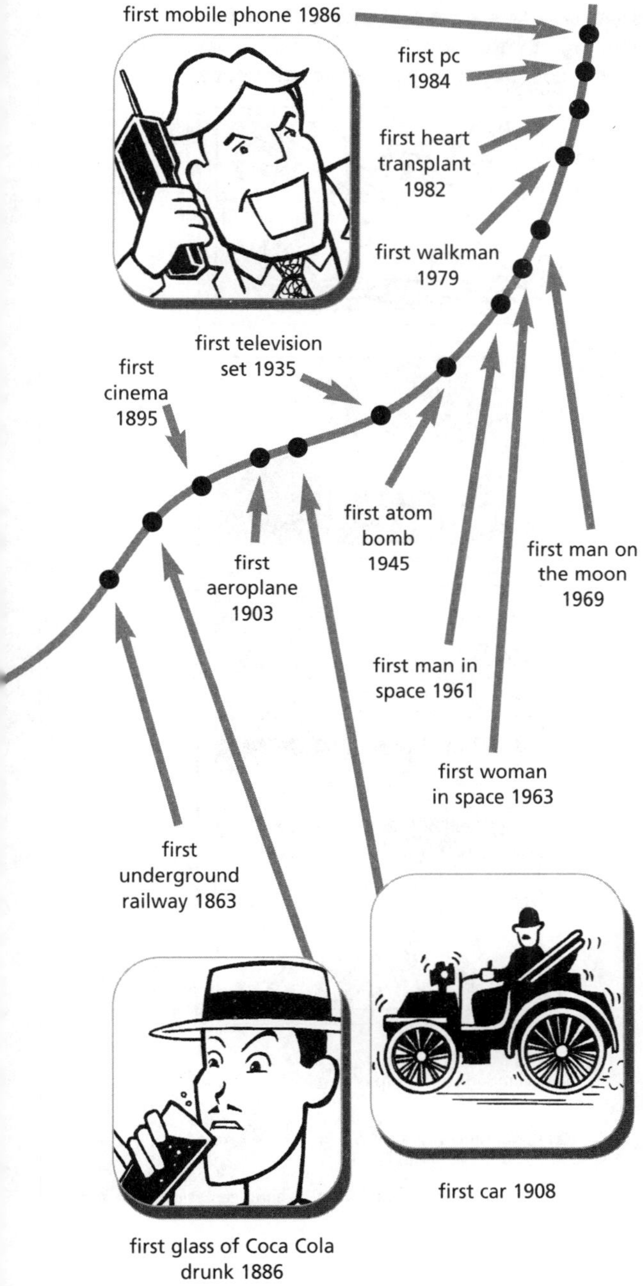

1. How long have humans lived on the earth?
(since) ______________________________

____

2. How long have people been painting pictures?
(since) ______________________________

____

3. How long have humans been in Europe?
(since) ______________________________

____

4. How long have people lived in cities?
(since) ______________________________

____

5. How long have people been farming?
(since) ______________________________

____

6. How long have people had books?
(for) ______________________________

____

7. How long have people been travelling by train?
(for) ______________________________

____

8. How long has Coca Cola been in the shops?
(for) ______________________________

____

9. How long have people had cars?
(for) ______________________________

____

10. How long have people had mobile phones?
(for) ______________________________

____

Here is Today's News

News readers on radio and television often use the present perfect to tell the day's news stories. These stories have got mixed up. First, sort out the sentences to make eight possible stories. Then, match the sentences to the pictures.

/f

1. The government f
2. Three dangerous crocodiles
3. A magician
4. A restaurant chef
5. Two schoolboys
6. Detectives
7. A vulture
8. A pet rat

a. have climbed to the top of the Millennium Wheel.
b. has saved his owners from a fire in their home.
c. have arrested two monkeys for stealing cameras at the zoo.
d. has crashed into an aeroplane at a height of 10,000 metres.
e. have escaped from the aquarium.
f. has introduced a new tax on chocolate.
g. has attacked his customers with a kitchen knife.
h. has lost his wife in a magic box.

A Fishy Story

Read the story and put the pictures in the order that they actually happened.

One strange day, fish fell out of the sky. It happened like this. I had gone to the shops to buy vegetables for supper and a bone for my dog. It wasn't raining when I left but I had taken my umbrella anyway. I got to the shops and bought the things I wanted. I was walking home when suddenly there was a loud bang and the sky went very dark. I looked up to see black shapes falling towards me. In an instant the shapes began to hit the ground. They hit me, too and knocked me over. They were fish. I was amazed. I looked around. Other people had come out into the street when they heard the noise. Nobody could explain it. That evening our street was on television. An old bomb from the war had exploded in the river that runs through the town. The bomb had lain at the bottom of the river for fifty years. So that night we had fish for supper with our vegetables.

a

b 1

c

d

e

f

g

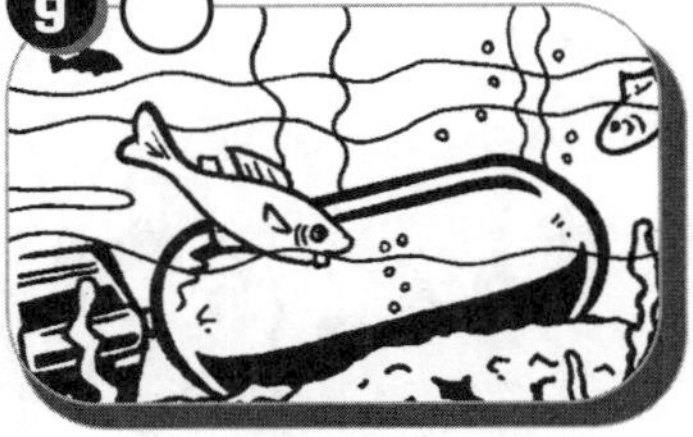

h

i

j

Trip to Town

You're going to town.

The time now is 9.50am. Your mum gives you this list.

return books
pay cheque into account
new trainers
haircut
buy: shampoo
toothpaste
large loaf
cakes for tea
buy stamps and post parcel

This is your list:

new CD
hire video for this evening
meet friends at burger bar 12.15

Add your own ideas:

....
....
....

This is what your mum says to you as you're going out of the door:

Remember the bank shuts at 12.00.

Don't forget the bakery sells out early.

Your hair appointment is at 11.30 - it'll take about half an hour.

Don't miss the 11 o'clock post.

Hurry up! You'll miss the bus. It leaves in 10 minutes.

BUS TIMETABLE

leaves	9.30	10.00	11.30
arrives	10.00	10.30	12.00

MUSIC / VIDEO MEGASTORE

LIBRARY
Opening hours
Mon-Sat 9.30-4.00

CYBER CAFE

The Bread Basket

cool shoes

The Hair Shop

Boots the chemist

POST OFFICE
Open Mon-Sat
9.00am - 5.30pm

On the bus you plan what you are going to do, using all the information on these pages.

Like this:

10.30 buy bread and cakes

10.45 post office

Then a friend gets on the bus. The time now is 10.15. He/She asks you what you're going to do today. Use words like these: *First, Next, Then, After that, Last*

Tell him/her, like this:

First, I'm going to buy some bread. Then, ...

What is Going to Happen Next?

Make eight predictions like this: *The little boy is going to fall into the hole.*

1. *The ants*
2. *The crocodile*
3. *The bridge*
4. *The swing*
5. *The bull*
6. *The monkey*
7. *The newspaper*
8. *The little dog*

Vote for Us

FIVE YEARS LATER…

1 No ______
2 ______
3 ______
4 ______
5 ______
6 ______
7 ______

Have the Forward Party's predictions come true? Read these newspaper stories and write *yes* or *no* in the spaces above.

STREET CRIME UP There were 40% more street crimes in the last three months.

NUMBERS OF WILD ANIMALS INCREASE
There are more hedgehogs, foxes, wild rabbits and badgers in our countryside than ever before.

'WHERE ARE OUR COMPUTERS?'
School teachers complained to the government yesterday that they had no computers in their classrooms.

MORE JOBS The number of employed people rose again last month.

FARM PROTEST
Hundreds of farmers drove their tractors around Parliament Square yesterday to protest against falling milk prices.

HOMES FOR THE POOR New houses for people on low incomes are now available.

TRAFFIC ISN'T MOVING
Drivers in Southampton city centre were angry yesterday when roadworks on the main roads caused hours of delay.

Emergency!

Do you know what to do in a crisis? Choose the correct answer.

1 If your friend has a nosebleed,
(a) you tell him to sit down and put his head between his knees.
(b) you tell him to stand on his head and drink a glass of water.
(c) you suddenly shout very loudly in his ear.

2 If the fire alarm goes off at school,
(a) you walk through the building and look for smoke and flames.
(b) you go outside and call the fire brigade.
(c) you don't do anything – it goes off all the time.

3 If a chemical spills in the science classroom at school,
(a) you wipe it up with a cloth.
(b) you find a teacher at once.
(c) you leave it – it will soon dry.

4 If you see a dog in the street with no owner and no collar,
(a) you catch it and stroke it.
(b) you don't do anything.
(c) you report it to the Council.

5 If you come home and smell gas,
(a) you switch the light on and check the house.
(b) you close the door and call the gas company from your neighbours' house.
(c) you don't worry about it.

6 If there is a fire in the kitchen,
(a) you stay in the room and open the windows.
(b) you go out of the room, close the door and call the fire brigade.
(c) you open all the doors in the house.

7 If you knock a tooth out in a football game,
(a) you wrap it up in a tissue and take it home.
(b) you put it under your tongue and go to your dentist.
(c) you put it in a glass of milk and go to your dentist.

8 If you cut your arm and it bleeds a lot,
(a) you hold your arm up in the air.
(b) you sit down and hold your arm up in the air.
(c) you lie down with your arm by your side.

9 If you find a burglar in your house,
(a) you try to catch him.
(b) you run out of the house and call for help.
(c) you offer him a cup of tea.

10 If you get hiccups,
(a) you put your head in a bucket.
(b) you stand on your head and drink a glass of water.
(c) you wait until they go.

April Fool

It's April 1st. Mr Jones, the English teacher, has left the classroom for a few minutes. His naughty students have decided to play some April Fool's tricks on him. Look at the picture and then fill in the missing words in the sentences below.

1 If h e opens t he door, t he flour w ______ fall o ______ his h ______ .

2 I ______ he l ______ in h ______ desk, a f ______ will j ______ out.

3 If h ______ sits d ______ , he w ______ stick t ______ his c ______ .

4 I ______ he w ______ on t ______ board, t ______ pen w ______ rub o ______ .

5 If h ______ plays t ______ cassette, h ______ will h ______ pop m ______ .

6 I ______ he o ______ his b ______ , he w ______ find a squashed t ______ .

7 If h ______ drinks h ______ coffee, i ______ will t ______ disgusting!

What Kind of Artist Are You?

We're all artistic, but we express ourselves in different ways. Do you express yourself best in pictures, music, words or with your body? First of all, fill in the gaps using the words in brackets to make second conditional sentences. Then, answer the questions and find out.

1 If you ______ (have) half an hour to spare now, what ______ (do)?

- **(a)** read a book
- **(b)** draw a picture
- **(c)** listen to some music
- **(d)** go outside and play football

2 If you ______ (go) to the theatre this evening, what ______ (choose) to see?

- **(a)** a ballet
- **(b)** a modern play
- **(c)** a Shakespeare play
- **(d)** a musical

3 If you ______ (go) to see your favourite band this evening, what ______ (do) in the half hour before you went?

- **(a)** worry about your clothes
- **(b)** listen to the band's CD
- **(c)** practise your dancing
- **(d)** find out facts about the band

4 If your English teacher ______ (ask) you to choose a fun class activity, which one ______ (choose)?

- **(a)** playing a game
- **(b)** watching a TV programme or film
- **(c)** listening to a song
- **(d)** discussion

5 If these teachers ______ (meet) your parents, who ______ (say) the nicest things about you?

- **(a)** your art teacher
- **(b)** your music teacher
- **(c)** your language teacher
- **(d)** your sports teacher

6 **Heroes....**

If you ______ (choose) one person to represent America, who ______ (choose)?

- **(a)** Michael Jordan
- **(b)** Madonna
- **(c)** Ernest Hemingway
- **(d)** Andy Warhol

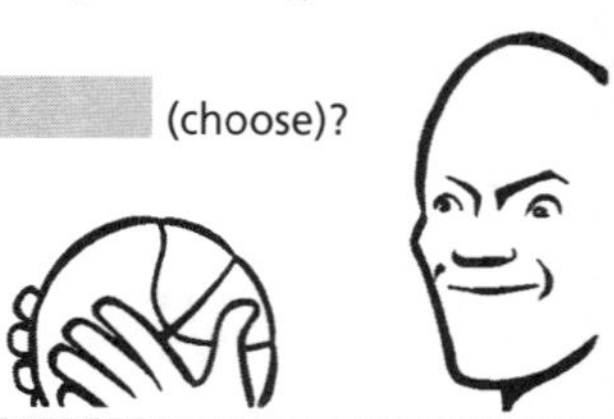

SCORES: 1a-4 1b-3 1c-2 1d-1; 2a-1 2b-3 2c-4 2d-2; 3a-3 3b-2 3c-1 3d-4; 4a-1 4b-3 4c-2 4d-4; 5a-3 5b-2 5c-4 5d-1; 6a-1 6b-2 6c-4 6d-3.

0-6 *You express yourself with your body* - you like to do things yourself rather than watch other people do them.

7-12 *Music comes first for you* - you are happiest when you are playing or listening to music.

13-18 *You are a visual person* - you always look first and find out information later.

19-24 *You are a words person* - you read about a painting before you look at it, you read about music before you listen to it.

What's It Made Of?

Use the words in the box to complete the sentences. Write the words in the puzzle. Find out what Jen's dress is made of.

glass metal rubber stone rope brick paper plastic ice wool

1. Books are made of ______________ .

2. The Eiffel Tower is made of ______________

3. These toys are made of ______________ .

4. The pyramids are made of ______________ .

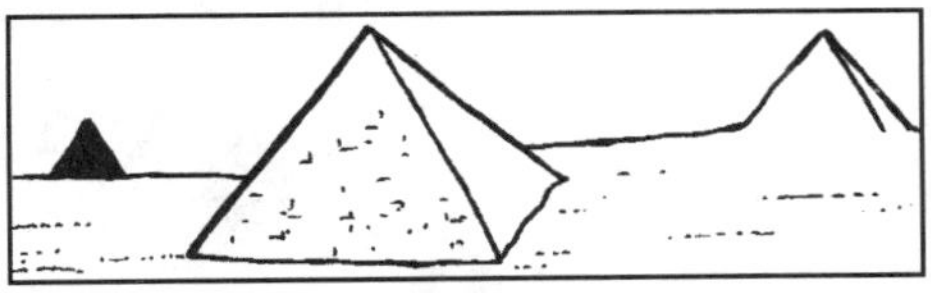

5. These tyres are made of ______________ .

6. Icebergs are made of ______________ .

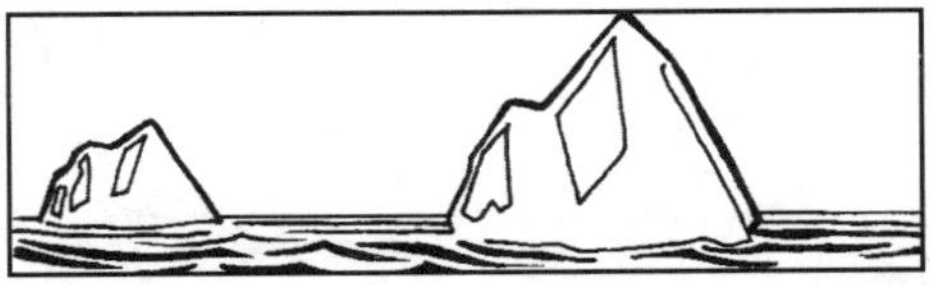

7. This jumper is made of ______________ .

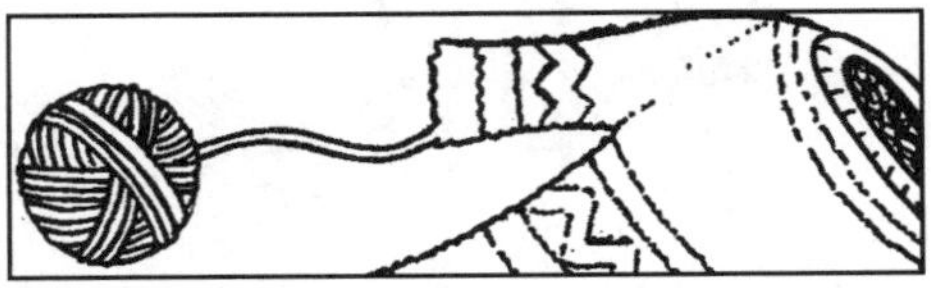

8. This wall is made of ______________ .

9. This swing is made of ______________ .

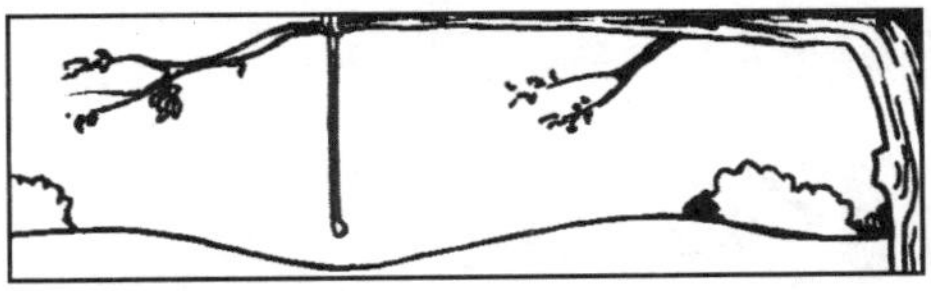

10. This bottle is made of ______________ .

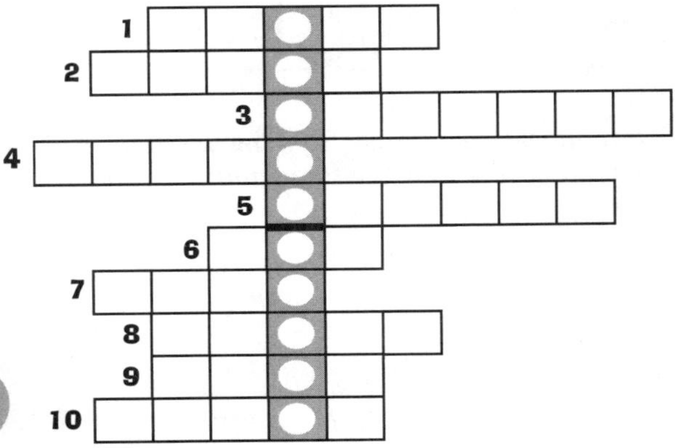

What's Happened to You?

What have these people had/got done? Complete the speech bubbles. Find the past participles you need in the wordsearch.

I	P	I	E	R	C	E	D
T	A	V	E	H	U	A	M
E	I	D	M	Y	T	P	E
S	N	H	O	T	T	O	N
T	T	G	R	A	A	P	D
E	E	H	T	K	A	K	E
D	D	D	Y	E	D	E	D
C	L	E	A	N	E	D	N

1

I've had my hair cut.

2

I've ______ my ______ ______

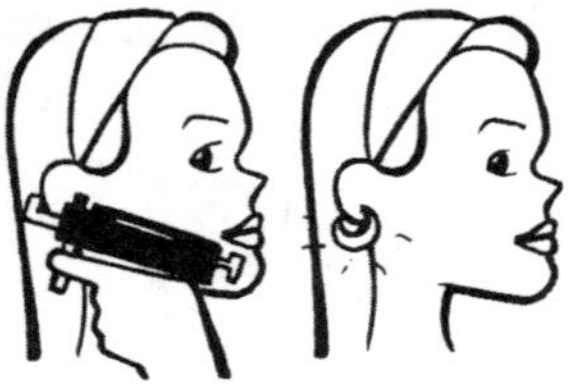

3

I've ______ my ______ ______

4

I've ______ my ______ ______

5

I've ______ my ______ ______ out!

6

We've ______ our ______ ______

7

I've ______ my ______ ______

8

I've ______ my ______ ______

Write the leftover letters from the wordsearch above to complete the sentence. Draw a picture to go with the sentence.

_'_ _

Answers

Page 4
Unchanging World
1 sleeps 2 sets 3 lasts
4 weighs, measures 5 loses
6 spends 7 throws, travels
8 drinks 9 closes 10 beats

Page 5
You're late!
The verbs appear in this form, in this order: waiting, leaving, 'm sitting, 'm getting out, 'm going into, running, falling into, 'm getting on, 're driving down, 'm pushing, 'm running out of

They are going to see *The Lion King*

Page 6
Where's Your Homework?
1 The dog ate it.
2 My computer exploded.
3 Some boys stole my school bag.
4 The queen came to tea.
5 Aliens landed in our garden and took my homework back to their planet.
6 An eagle took my homework and used it to make a nest.
7 My brother made a paper plane with it.
8 My father lit the fire with it.
9 A professor thought it was brilliant and took it back to his university.

Page 7
Michael Johnson
1 broke 2 was 3 seemed
4 studied 5 realised 6 said
7 signed 8 won 9 retired

He studied *marketing.*

Page 8
Amazon Diary
a5 b8 c7 d3 e1 f2
g6 h4

He met four types of creature: ants, piranha fish, a crocodile and a monkey.

Page 9
Pompeii
1 He was drinking a glass of wine at the bar.
2 They were buying loaves and honey cakes.
3 They were playing a game with stones in the road.
4 She was writing a letter.
5 They were painting pictures of the countryside on the walls.
6 It was sleeping in the corner.
7 He grabbed Agrippa's hand and ran out of the house.
8 It hid under the table.
9 The children cried for their parents.
10 Most of them escaped but two thousand died.

Pages 10 and 11
Memory Test
1 She was climbing a mountain.
2 He was having a shower.
3 They were swimming in the sea.
4 At 8.30 yesterday evening.
5 At 4.00 this afternoon.
6 She was riding a horse on the beach.
7 He was working on his computer.
8 At 4.00 this afternoon.
9 They were shopping.
10 He was ice skating.

Pages 12 and 13
That's History!
1 Since 100,000 BC.
2 Since 20,000 BC
3 Since 40,000 BC.
4 Since 4,000 BC.
5 Since 8,000 BC.
6 For about 555 years.
7 For about 178 years.
8 For about 118 years.
9 For more than 90 years.
10 For more than 16 years.

Page 14
Here is Today's News
1f 2e 3h 4g 5a 6c
7d 8b

Page 15
A Fishy Story
1b 2i 3c 4f 5j 6h 7a
8e 9g 10d

Pages 16 and 17
Trip to Town
This is one possible plan:

10.30	buy bread and cakes (remember the baker sells out early)
10.45	post office (don't miss the 11 o'clock post)
11.00	bank (they shut at 12.00)

11.15	chemist (just time to buy shampoo and toothpaste)
11.30	hairdresser's
12.00	library
12.15	coffee with friends
1.00	Music/Video Megastore
1.30	Shoe shop
2.00	go home

Page 18
What is Going to Happen Next?

Suggested answers:

The ants are going to steal/take the picnic.
The crocodile is going to eat the duck.
The bridge is going to break.
The swing is going to break.
The bull is going to push the woman over.
The monkey is going to steal/take the buns.
The newspaper is going to catch fire.
The little dog is going to steal/take the big dog's bone.

Page 19
Vote for Us

Yes: protect the countryside, create more jobs, build new and cheap houses
No: reduce crime, help farmers, prepare our young people for the future, modernise our transport system.

Page 20
Emergency!

The correct answers:

1 a-4 He can pinch the top of his nose at the same time; b-0 that's for hiccups; c-0
2 a-0 No! Go straight outside; b-4; c-0
3 a-0 Don't touch it; b-4; c-0 It might be dangerous.
4 a-0 It might bite you; b-0; c-4
5 a-0 The light switch can cause an explosion; b-4; c-0 Always report a smell of gas
6 a-0; b-4; c-0
7 a-0 If it dries, it can't be put back in; b-4; c-4 You can try and put it back in yourself on the way to the dentist but keep it WET.
8 a-2, b-4, c-0 The bleeding stops of you hold it up – get help as well.
9 a-0; b-4; c-0
10 a-0; b-2 Some people think this works; c-2 Is there a cure for hiccups?

Your score

0-20 I won't come to you in an emergency!
21-30 Pretty good score, but maybe you should take a Safety First of r First Aid course.
31-40 Do you work for the emergency services?

Page 21
April Fool

1 If he opens the door, the flour will fall on his head.
2 If he looks in his desk, a frog will jump out.
3 If he sits down, he will stick to his chair.
4 If he writes on the board, the pen won't rub out.
5 If he plays the cassette, he will hear pop music.
6 If he opens his book, he will find a squashed tomato.
7 If he drinks his coffee, it will taste disgusting.

Page 22
What Kind of Artist Are You?

1 had; would you do 2 went; would you choose 3 went; would you do 4 asked; would you choose 5 met; would say 6 chose; would you choose

Page 23
What's It Made Of?

1 paper 2 metal 3 plastic 4 stone 5 rubber 6 ice 7 wool 8 brick 9 rope 10 glass
It's made of *paper clips*.

Page 24
What's Happened To You?

1 I've had my hair cut.
2 I've had my ears pierced.
3 I've had my hair dyed black.
4 I've had my car mended.
5 I've had my tooth taken out.
6 We've had our windows cleaned.
7 I've had my eyes tested.
8 I've had my face painted.

I	P	I	E	R	C	E	D
T	A	V	E	H	U	A	M
E	I	D	M	Y	T	P	E
S	N	H	O	T	T	O	N
T	T	G	R	A	A	P	D
E	E	H	T	K	A	K	E
D	D	D	Y	E	D	E	D
C	L	E	A	N	E	D	N

I've had my photograph taken.

Page 25
Great Natural Disasters

A When Mt Vesuvius erupted in AD79, the Roman town of Pompeii was buried under a

mountain of ash.
B A fire started in Pudding Lane in London in 1666 and the city of London was burnt to the ground.
C When the Titanic hit an iceberg in 1912, over 1,000 people were lost in the icy waters of the Atlantic Ocean.
D In the Great Fire of 1871 in Chicago, the iron skyscrapers were melted to the ground by the heat.
E After a terrible earthquake in Portugal in 1775, the city of Lisbon was hit by 15-metre-high waves.

Page 26
Zak's Coffee Bar
1 must 2 mustn't 3 mustn't 4 must 5 mustn't 6 must 7 mustn't 8 must 9 must 10 must

Page 27
School's Out
Alan – a Beth – a Chris – b Diana – a Ewan – a Flyn – a Gill – b Harry – a
Chris and Flyn will need their swimming costumes. (Gill, Ewan, Beth and Diana are going bowling; Alan and Harry are going to a café.)

Page 28
Our Bodies
1 to breathe 2 to run 3 to stand up 4 to chew 5 to eat 6 to see 7 to balance 8 to write and draw 9 to store 10 to pump
A5 B9 C6 D4 E10 F1 G3 H8 I2 J7

Page 29
To: Ben@astro.co.uk
1 won't there? 2 will you? 3 can we? 4 doesn't she? 5 aren't you? 6 can't we? 7 can you?
The correct order is:
c, g, e, j, b, f, a, i, d, h

Page 30
Alien Language
They told me that they had crashed into the sea. They thought their spaceship would go rusty.
Deff said he needed uranium to mend their spaceship.
Then XrT1 asked what that funny smell was.
Deff wanted to know if they could phone home.

Page 31
Tropical Island
The correct choices spell *plane crash.*

Pages 32 and 33
Word Chain
1 mobile phone 2 electric socket 3 textbook 4 keyhole 5 egg cup 6 paper clip 7 plant pot 8 traffic lights 9 sunglasses 10 steering wheel 11 light switch 12 hairbrush 13 handbag 14 girlfriend 15 day dream

Page 34
This Creature is Weird
It has a tiger's head, a chicken's body, an elephant's legs and a peacock's tail.
1 It has a fish's head, a giraffe's body, an eagle's legs and an eagle's tail.
2 It has a monkey's head, an elephant's body, a pig's legs and a fish's tail.
3 It has an eagle's head, a monkey's body, a giraffe's legs and a pig's tail.
4 It has a snake's head, a fish's body, a tortoise's legs and a monkey's tail.
5 It has a pig's head, a tortoise's body, a peacock's legs and an elephant's tail.

Page 35
Lost Property
1 children's 2 alien's 3 dogs' 4 mice's 5 magician's 6 old woman's 7 football player's 8 chefs'

Pages 36 and 37
These Clothes Don't Fit
1 Lara – trousers
2 Emily – shoes
3 Isobel – skirt
4 Ned – scarf
5 Sam – schoolbag
6 Geri – socks
7 Harry – sunglasses

Pages 38 and 39
Is Anybody There?
1 Somebody – B
2 somewhere – E
3 Everybody – A
4 nowhere, nowhere – H
5 anybody – C
6 anywhere – G
7 nobody – D
8 Nothing – F

Page 40
City or Country?
1 a lot of (I)
2 There is (F)
3 There are (T)
4 not enough (F)
5 hardly any (Y)
6 too much (T)
7 hardly any (K)

8 There are (O)
9 plenty of (Y)
10 There is (O)
Nearly *fifty* per cent of the world's population lives in cities and the largest in the world is *Tokyo.*

Page 41
At the Olympics

Today (t) First (h) here (e)
fast (t) Unluckily (o) ready (r)
early (t) extremely (o)
slowly (i) apparently (s)
ever (e)
The animal is 3, *the tortoise*.

Page 42 and 43
Comparing Animals

1) 1, 4, 7 and 8 are false.
2, 3, 5 and 6 are true.
2) 1 The giant squid is nearly as long as the whale shark.
2 The ostrich is as fast as the emu.
3 The grey whale is half as long as the blue whale.
4 The Andean condor is a lot lighter than a moose.
5 The blue whale is much longer than a Komodo dragon.

Page 44
The Biggest and the Best

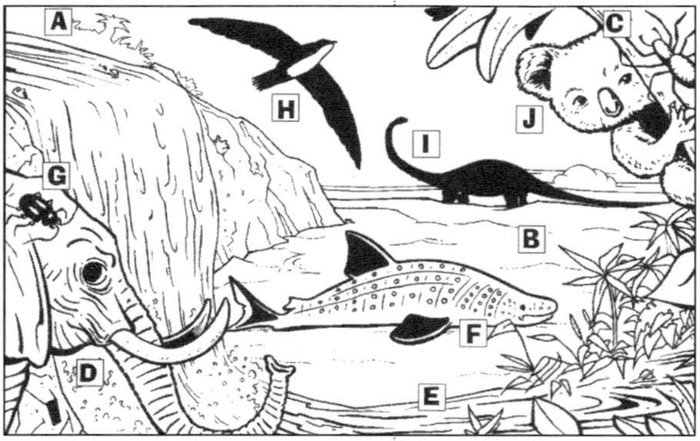

1 highest 2 largest 3 deadliest
4 heaviest 5 deepest
6 heaviest 7 commonest
8 fastest 9 biggest
10 sleepiest

Page 45
Robbie, the School Rabbit

1 a 2 a 3 the 4 the 5 the
6 the 7 the 8 the 9 the
10 a 11 an 12 the 13 the
14 the 15 a 16 a 17 the
18 The 19 The 20 the 21 the
22 the 23 the 24 the 25 the

Pages 46 and 47
Treasure Hunt

The treasure is *chocolate*.

Great Natural Disasters

Put the pictures in order. Put the missing verbs in the captions in the past simple passive. Choose the verbs from the box.

hit bury melt burn drown

A

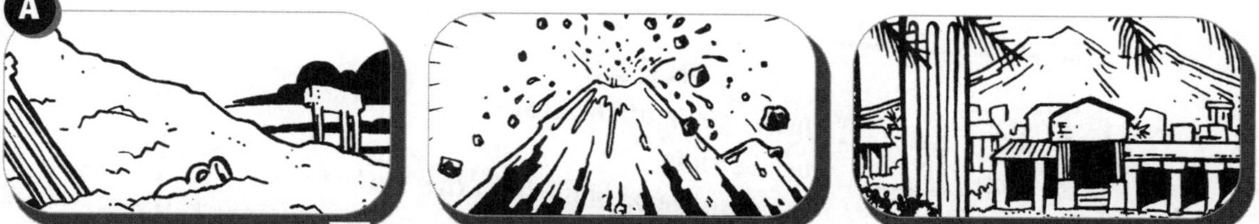

under a mountain of ash. 3

When Mt Vesuvius erupted in AD79,

the Roman town of Pompeii ______________

B

the city of London

______________ to the ground.

A fire started in Pudding Lane in London in 1666 and

C

When the Titanic hit an iceberg in 1912,

over 1,500 people ______________

in the icy waters of the Atlantic Ocean.

D

the iron skyscrapers ______________

to the ground by the heat.

In the Great Fire of 1871 in Chicago,

E

by 15-metre-high waves.

After a terrible earthquake in Portugal in 1775,

the city of Lisbon ______________

Zak's Coffee Bar

Zak has a new girl working for him on Saturdays. He shows her the list of rules. Write *must* or *mustn't* in the gaps.

RULES

1. You __________ always smile at the customers.
2. You __________ ever be rude.
3. There __________ be a queue of more than five customers.
4. The tables __________ always be cleaned before a new customer sits down.
5. Customers __________ smoke in the non-smoking areas.
6. You __________ sweep the floor every half hour.
7. You __________ eat or drink while you are working.
8. You __________ ask people who don't buy anything to leave.
9. Coffee and tea __________ always be served really hot.
10. Long hair __________ be tied back.

Here's the cafe at lunchtime. Which rules are being broken?

Write the numbers in the boxes. [ ] [ ] [ ] [ ] [ ]

School's Out

We're free! What shall we do?
Each friend has a different suggestion about what to do. Can you decide which option makes a correct grammatical sentence? Check your answer by following the line. If you find the right picture, your answer is correct.

Alan

Shall we ...
a) play by the river?
b) playing by the

Beth

Let's ...
a) see a film
b) seeing a film

Chris

How about ...
a) go shopping?
b) going shopping?

Diana

Why don't we...
a) go bowling?
b) to go bowling?

Ewan

What about ...?
a) riding our bikes
b) ride our bikes

Flynn

We could ...
a) go for a swim
b) swimming

Gill

Would you like ...?
a) visit the zoo
b) to visit the zoo

Harry

I think we should ...
a) go to a café
b) to go to a café

Gill, Ewan and Beth decide to go with Diana.
Alan decides to go with Harry.
Chris decides to go with Flynn.
So who will need their swimming costumes?

Our Bodies

Find the right verb to complete these sentences. Write the numbers of the sentences in the correct place on the picture.

to breathe to stand up to write and draw to pump
to chew to see to eat to balance to run to store

1 We need our lungs ____________

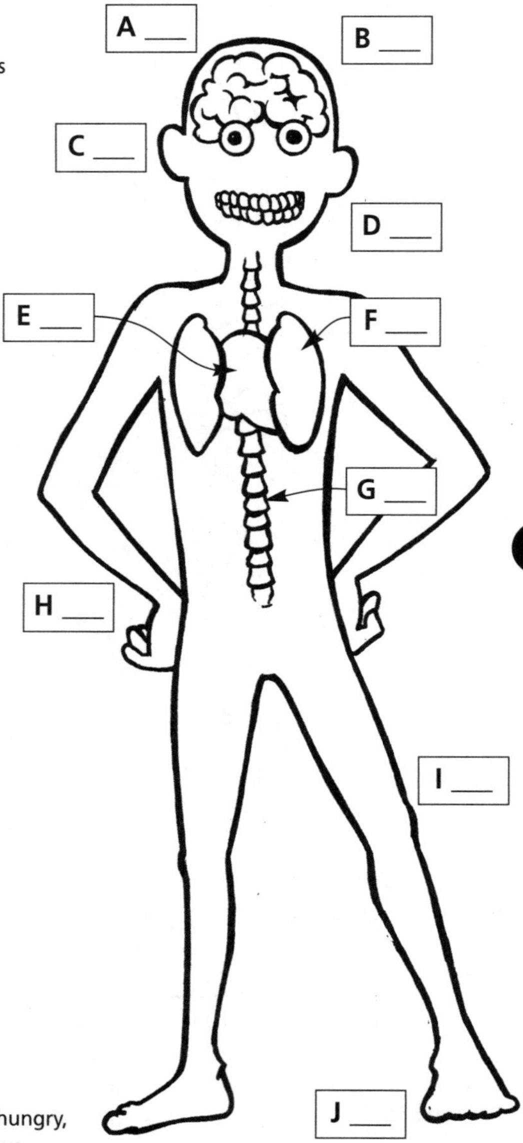

2 Our leg muscles help us ____________

3 We need our spine ____________ straight.

4 We use our teeth ____________ our food.

5 When we are hungry, our brain tells us ____________

6 Our eyes allow us ____________

7 We use our toes and ears ____________

8 The 27 bones in our hands help us ____________

9 We use our memory ____________ information.

10 We need our heart ____________ blood around our body.

To: Ben@astro.co.uk

Ben and Jan are with their class in the computer room. Their teacher, Miss Jones, is there too. Miss Jones thinks they are doing their homework. They're actually having an email conversation.

1. **Write the question tags in the spaces.**
2. **Put the messages in the right order in the boxes.**

To: Ben@astro.co.uk

Subject: the beach

a. But suppose we see them on the beach. Then there'll be trouble, (1)...........?

b. Sure, Ben. But you won't be able to come, (2)............?

c. We can't go to the beach this weekend, (3).............?

d. Mrs J thinks we're doing our homework, (4).............?

e. You're going to your cousins' house, (5).............?

To: Jan@whistlejacket.co.uk

Subject: Sea and sand

f. Well, perhaps I can come. I can tell my mum that you're ill in bed and I have to visit you. Then we can go to the beach, (6)...........?

g. Why can't we?

h. No, Jan, she doesn't. She's standing right behind you.

i. I know. I'll say that you need the sea air because you're ill.

j. No, I'm not. They're coming to see us instead. Help! You can't invite me to your house, (7).............?

SEND

c									

Alien Language

You and your friend Sam are out late one afternoon. It's just getting dark. Suddenly a group of aliens appears in front of you. They speak in their language. Strangely, you can understand it, but Sam can't.

ALIEN CODE

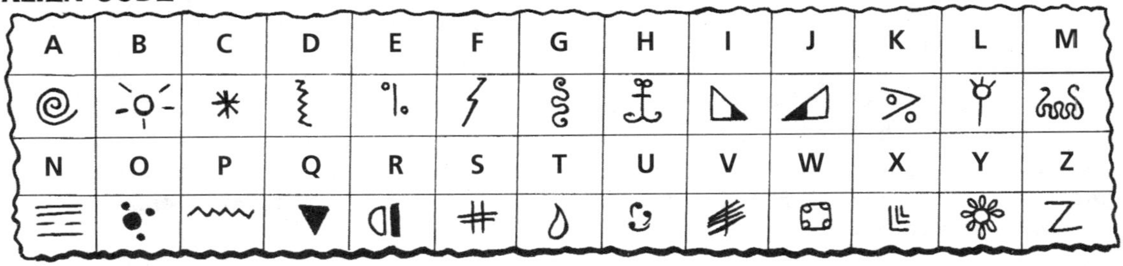

After they've gone, Sam wants to know what they said. Tell him.

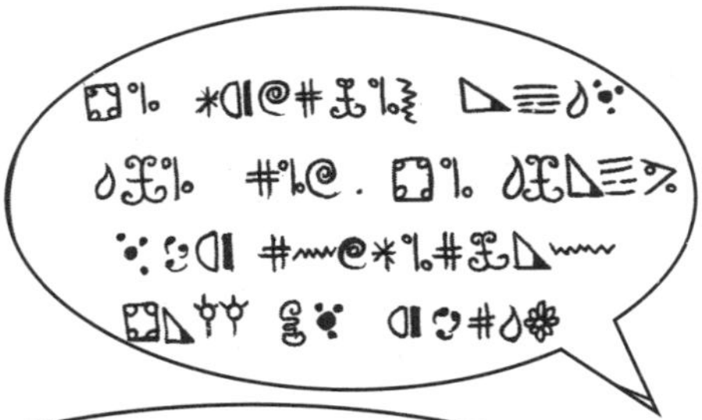

They told me that ....

....

....

....

Deff said ....

....

....

....

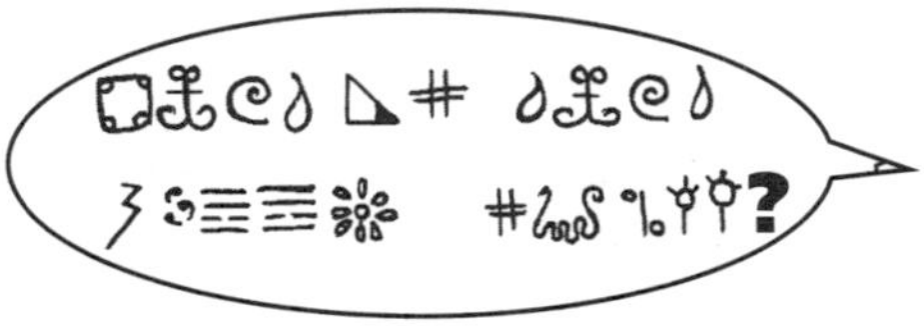

XrTl asked ....

....

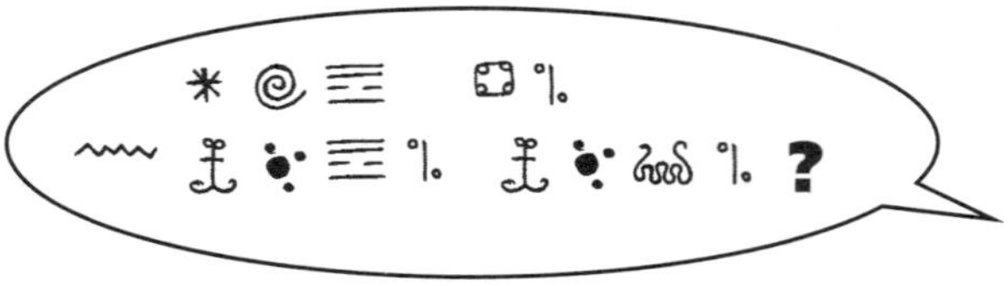

Deff wanted to know if

....

....

Tropical Island

Some people arrived on a tropical island. A few weeks later they were rescued. Follow the sentence paths to read their story. When you choose between some and any, write the letter in the spaces at the bottom of the page to find out how they first arrived on the island.

There weren't p any some b people on the island.

They slept on o any some l leaves and branches on the first night.

They found a some any l fruit but they didn't find e some n any fresh water.

They made a fire with e some any p sticks.

They made friends with some c f any monkeys.

The monkeys showed them r some any s coconut trees.

They didn't have f some any a hope of rescue.

s Some Any z people in a boat saw h some any t smoke from their fire.

_ _ _ _ _   _ _ _ _ _

Word Chain

1 **Complete the name of the things in the pictures. Use the words in the box to form compound nouns.**

bag	friend	phone
book	glasses	pot
brush	hole	socket
clip	dream	switch
cup	lights	wheel

1 mobile ....

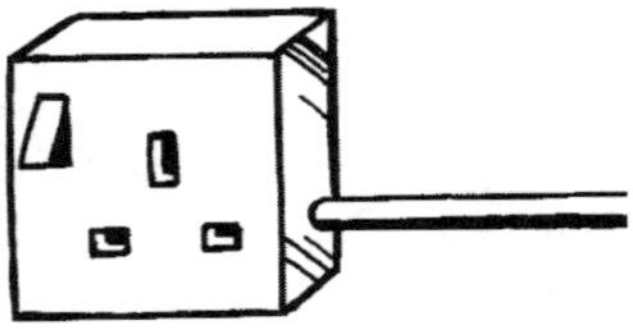

2 electric ....

3 text ....

4 key ....

5 egg ....

6 paper ....

7 plant ....

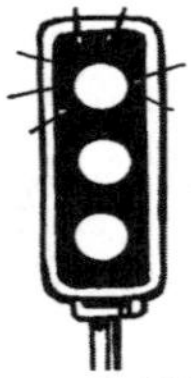

8 traffic ....

9 sun ....

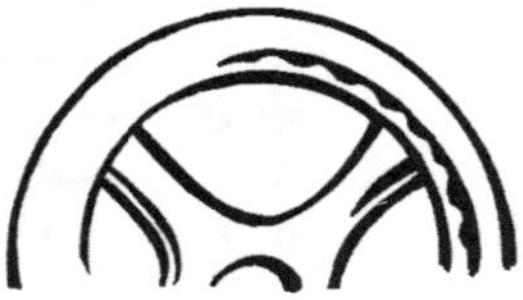

10 steering ....

11 light ....

12 hair ....

13 hand ....

14 girl ....

15 day ....

2 Write the words in the word chain.
The last letter of a word is the first letter of the next word.

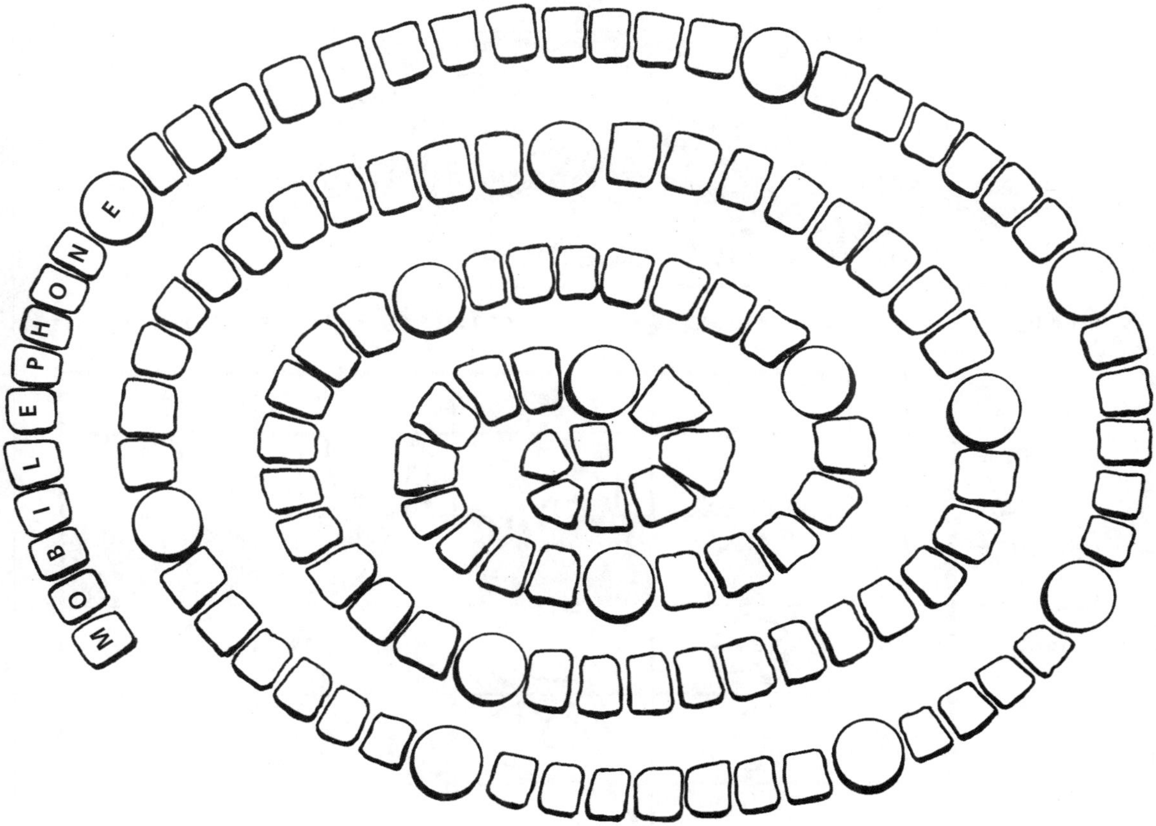

3 How many more compound nouns can you make?
Use the words in the box and continue the list.

school bag, address book, clothes brush,

This Creature is Weird

Look at the picture and fill in the missing words in the description below.

It has a tiger's ________ , a chicken's ________ , an elephant's ________ and a peacock's ________ .

GIRAFFE
PEACOCK
MONKEY
TORTOISE
ELEPHANT
FISH
PIG
SNAKE
EAGLE

HEAD
BODY
LEGS
TAIL

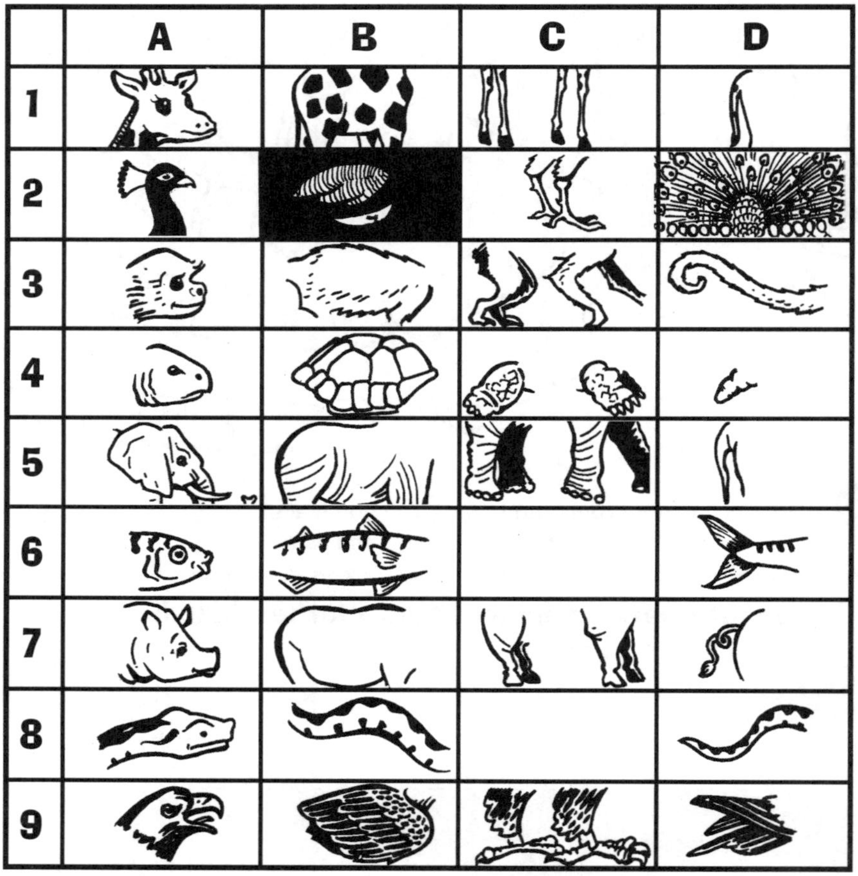

Draw and describe these weird creatures.

1. A6, B1, C9, D9 It ______________________
2. A3, B5, C7, D6 It ______________________
3. A9, B3, C1, D7 It ______________________
4. A8, B6, C4, D3 It ______________________
5. A7, B4, C2, D5 It ______________________

Lost Property

There's a queue at the Lost Property Office. Can you help the man match the people to their lost items? Write your answers in the sentences below.

1. They are the __________ toys.
2. It's the __________ map.
3. They are the __________ bones.
4. It's the __________ cheese.
5. It's the __________ pointed hat.
6. It's the __________ walking stick.
7. It's the __________ football.
8. They are the __________ hats.

These Clothes Don't Fit!

These children are all in the same class. The head teacher is checking their school uniform.

Read what the head teacher says and write the correct name in the box next to each child.

Sam, your shirt is too scruffy!

Lara, your shoes are too tight!

Harry, your trousers are too short!

Emily, your skirt is too long!

Ned, your scarf is too long!

Geri, your boots are too big!

Isobel, your jacket is too small!

What is it?

Read the sentences. What does *one* or *ones* refer to in each sentence?

Harry has large round ones.

Isobel has a striped one.

Emily has black ones.

Ned has a striped one.

Sam has a large one.

Geri has white ones.

Lara has striped ones.

Is Anybody There?

Use the words in the box to complete the conversations.

nobody	**everybody**	**anybody**	**somebody**
nowhere	**nothing**	**anywhere**	**somewhere**

1

2

3

4

5

6

7

8

Now find the next line of each conversation.

A Oh no! I'm going out, then.

B You get it!

C NNNNOOOOOOOOHHHHHHHHHH!

D Maybe somebody's left a message on my mobile phone.

E You said that three hours ago!

F Perhaps the dog ate it.

G No, there aren't!

H But he has got a big brother.

City or Country?

What do city kids and country kids think about their lives? Complete the speech bubbles with words from the box.

a lot of (I)   There is (F)   not enough (F)   hardly any (Y)   There are (T)

hardly any (K)   There is (O)   too much (T)   plenty of (Y)   There are (O)

Nearly _ _ _ _ _ (2 1 4 3 5) per cent of the world's population live in cities and the largest city in the world is _ _ _ _ _ (6 10 7 9 8).

At the Olympics

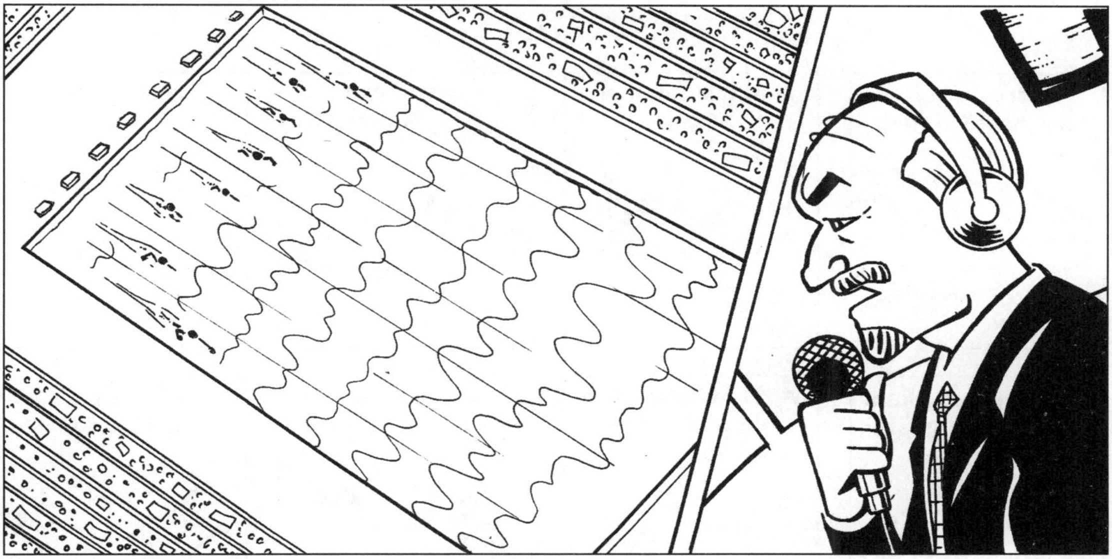

The adverbs in these sentences are mixed up. Put them in the correct sentences.

today — Unluckily (o) is another very exciting day at the Olympics.

Slowly (i) we go to the Olympic swimming pool.

Extremely (o) is the young swimmer that everybody is talking about.

He swims as today (t) and as elegantly as a dolphin.

Ever (e) for us, his race has just finished.

But they are first (h) to begin the next race.

Only three swimmers in this race. They're off! Oh no! A false start. Two of the swimmers dived in too fast (t). They are disqualified. That leaves only one swimmer in the pool. Has this ever happened before?

Off he goes. He seems to be swimming apparently (s) early (t).

Here (e) he has never swum in a 50-metre pool before. He only learned to swim a year ago!

Is he going to finish the race? Yes! In the slowest time ready (r)!

Write the letter attached to each adverb here:

T _ _   _ _ _ _ _ _ _ _

Which of these animals did the swimmer remind people of?

1

2

3

4

Comparing Animals

a grey whale can be 15m long

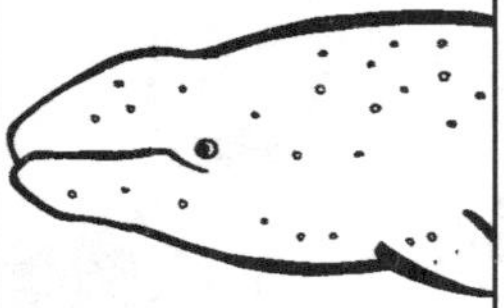

an ostrich can run 65km/h

a whale shark can be 18m long

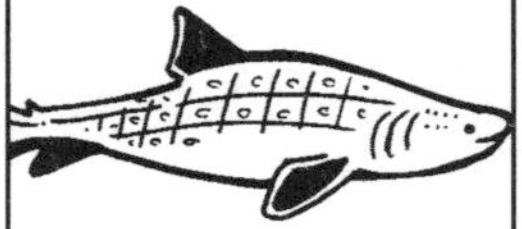

a puma can jump 5m high

an Arican elephant can live 60 years

a Komodo dragon can be 3m long

an Andean condor can weigh 12 kilos

a giant squid can be 17m long

a cheetah can run 100 km/h

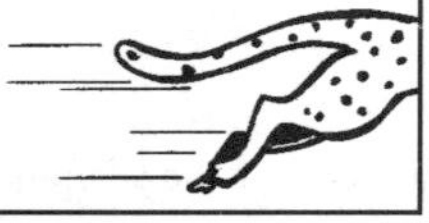

a bee hummingbird can weigh 1.4 grams

a mexican road-runner can run 45 km/h

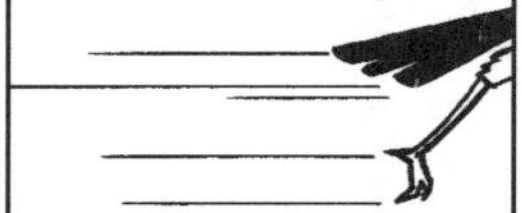

a polar bear can weigh 324 kilos

an albatross can live for 70 years

an emu can run 65 km/h

a blue whale can weigh 155,963 kilos

an antelope can jump 3m high

a blue whale can be 30m long

a dolphin can live for 60 years

a gazelle can run 90 km/h

a moose can weigh 362 kilos

1. Use the animal facts to help you decide if these sentences are true or false.

1	A bee hummingbird can weigh as much as a polar bear.	**True**	**False**
2	An African elephant can live just as long as a dolphin.	**True**	**False**
3	A polar bear can weigh nearly as much as a moose.	**True**	**False**
4	A cheetah can run twice as fast as a gazelle.	**True**	**False**
5	A Mexican road-runner can run half as fast as a gazelle.	**True**	**False**
6	A puma can jump higher than an antelope.	**True**	**False**
7	A whale shark can be a lot longer than a grey whale.	**True**	**False**
8	A giant squid can't be as long as a Komodo dragon.	**True**	**False**

2. Write sentences using the words in the box and the information on page 42.

a lot ______ er than
nearly as ______ as
much ______ er than
as ______ as
half as ______ as

1. **giant squid / whale shark** ______________________________
2. **ostrich / emu** ______________________________
3. **grey whale / blue whale** ______________________________
4. **Andean condor / a moose** ______________________________
5. **blue whale / Komodo dragon** ______________________________

The Biggest and the Best!

**These are some of the biggest, the highest, and the best in the world.
First label the pictures.**

**A. Angel Falls B. Sahara desert C. banana spider D. African elephant E. Amazon River
F. whale shark G. beetle H. swift I. Seismosaurus J. koala bear**

**Use the adjectives in the box to make superlatives about each picture.
Put them in the sentences below.**

heavy x2
large
sleepy
deep
common
high
deadly
fast
big

1. Angel Falls in Venezuela is the ______ waterfall in the world.
2. The Sahara is the ______ desert in the world.
3. The banana spider is the ______ there is.
4. The African elephant is the ______ animal on land.
5. The Amazon is the ______ river in the Americas.
6. The whale shark is the ______ shark in the oceans.
7. The beetle is the ______ insect in the world.
8. The swift is the ______ bird in the air.
9. The Seismosaurus was the ______ dinosaur on earth.
10. The koala bear is the ______ animal in the world.

Robbie, the School Rabbit

Put *the* or *a / an* in the spaces in the story below.

Once upon (1) ________ time, on (2) ________ boring Wednesday afternoon, Jed and Jen decided to steal Robbie, (3) ________ school rabbit. They took it home. At (4) ________ time, they thought it was funny.
But (5) ________ next day, (6) ________ head teacher told (7) ________ whole school and everyone was very sad. Jed and Jen were sad, too.
"We'll have to put it back," said Jen. "But nobody must see us."

So that evening, they took (8) ________ rabbit back. They carried (9) ________ rabbit in (10) ________ box. At school there was (11) ________ evening class going on, so (12) ________ school building was open. They crept in. They walked quickly down (13) ________ main corridor. There were lots of doors into classrooms and (14) ________ library. They turned the corner.

Suddenly they heard (15) ________ noise behind them - footsteps coming towards the corner. They ran into (16) ________ classroom and hid. Jed put (17) ________ box down. They waited. (18) ________ footsteps walked away.
"Come on," whispered Jed. "Let's go."
"Oh no!" said Jen, too loudly. "(19) ________ rabbit's gone."

They rushed back into (20) ________ corridor. They were just in time to see (21) ________ rabbit hop into (22) ________ main school hall. They ran to (23) ________ hall but stopped suddenly. (24) ________ hall was full of people speaking French. It was (25) ________ French evening class.

Treasure Hunt

Follow the path to the treasure. Collect the letters on the way.

The first letter is **on** a straight path.

The second letter is **next to** a prickly bush.

The third letter is **in** a shark's mouth.

The fourth letter is **above** a triangular hole in the castle wall.

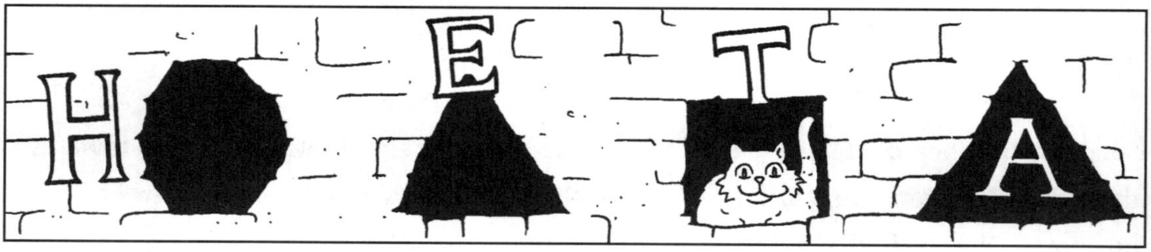

The fifth letter is **in front of** a narrow window halfway up a tower.

The sixth letter is **on top of** an octagonal tower.

The seventh letter is **behind** a tall, thin guard.

The eighth letter is **to the left of** a wooden box.

The ninth letter is **underneath** the striped cat.

Write your letters here. _ _ _ _ _ _ _ _ _

Sort them out to find the treasure. _ _ _ _ _ _ _ _ _

CLUE (The treasure will disappear quickly when you find it.)

Material written by: **Jane Rollason**

Project Editor: **Judith Greet**

Designers: **Alison Bond**, **Caroline Grimshaw**

Cover Design: **Kaya-anne Cully**

Illustrations by: **Carl Flint**

Photo: (Page 7) Wally Mcnamee / Corbis

Mary Glasgow Magazines, an imprint of Scholastic Inc., 2003

Printed in the UK by Ashford Colour Press Ltd, Gosport, Hampshire